30 DAY

WHOLE FOOD

SLOW COOKER

CHALLENGE

Whole Food Slow Cooker Recipes

Pictures, Serving, and Nutrition Facts for Every Recipe! Fast and Easy Approved Whole Foods Recipes for Weight Loss

By: Austin Ludwig

1

Legal notice

30 DAY WHOLE FOOD SLOW COOKER CHALLENGE

30 DAY WHOLE FOOD SLOW COOKER CHALLENGE

30 DAY WHOLE FOOD SLOW COOKER CHALLENGE

Introduction

The Whole Food 30 day challenge is a month long program that promotes clean eating and healthy living. The idea behind the diet is that certain types of foods, such as those that are heavily processed, have a negative impact on our health. Unfortunately, these processed "Franken-foods" are what a large majority of Americans and other western nations consume on regular basis. Doing a Whole Food challenge means you are challenging yourself to eat and live the way nature intended by excluding processed ingredients, additives, alcohol, and artificial sweeteners from all of your meals. Just by eliminating these foods from their diets for only one month often has such a dramatic impact on feelings of health, energy, and mental focus, that those who dare to try the 30 day Whole Food challenge end up becoming life-long converts.

Doing a Whole Food 30 day challenge and ultimately living a Whole Food lifestyle is not specifically aimed at losing weight, but rather that promoting the maximum quality of life. Inevitably however, eating fresh, tasty, Whole Food meals at home results in losing fat quickly, sometimes in significant quantities! When you eat the way nature intended, you will also start to look the way nature intended, which is lean and mean, not fat, slow and lethargic.

In addition to avoiding the forbidden foods, there is one other important rule to follow during your 30 day challenge: you must not weigh yourself at all during the next 30 days. Avoiding the scale for a month will not only end your obsession with your weight but will also keep those negative thoughts about your weight at bay. Remember that the focus of the challenge isn't just the number you see when you look down at the scale. It is about feeling young and energetic. It is about being proud of the way you live and the way you look. It is about *living well*.

The point of the Whole Food challenge is to teach you how to eat well and break all those unhealthy habits that prevent your body from being properly nourished. Moreover, avoiding the processed and forbidden foods while enjoying the abundance of healthy, fresh, and delicious Whole Foods will help improve your metabolism and help your body stop relying on low quality energy sources like sugar and refined carbs. Instead, the body will burn more fat, and you will get slimmer while feeling better than you have in years.

How are such changes possible?

Exposing our bodies regularly to the negative influences of processed foods may cause gut disruptions, inflammation, and hormone imbalances, as well as a variety of other maladies that can seriously impact the quality of our lives as well as our longevity. Moreover, they slow down our metabolism and prevent our bodies from using the nutrients they need in an efficient way. When we stop consuming the unhealthy junk that permeates the Standard American Diet (the acronym spells SAD for a reason!), the body will be rejuvenated and reenergized by finally getting the nutrients it wants and needs. You might notice many changes during your 30 day challenge, such as positive changes to your skin and hair. They will be glowing and shiny because of the vitamins and other nutrients they are finally getting access to.

Living a Whole Food lifestyle will also help to improve your athletic performance and make you feel more energetic as well. When you are used to consuming a Standard American Diet, your body has been getting most of its energy from refined carbs and sugar. When you start your 30 day Whole Food challenge, you may feel a bit sluggish until your body adapts to the new fuel sources. After a week or so, when your body gets used to your new diet, you will notice a big spike in your energy levels that will enable you to work out harder or maintain any activity for longer than you were previously able to.

You will likely notice your sleep patterns improving over the course of your 30 day challenge as well. The science behind this says that healthy eating, and especially avoiding excessive sugar and highly processed carbohydrates, helps regulate hormone levels and eliminate any hormone imbalances. Your body will shut down more easily at the end of the day, entering a deep and restorative sleep, and waking up feeling rested and refreshed.

What foods to eat?

The 30 day Whole Food challenge is easy to follow. You just have to stick to the Whole Food rules for a month without cheating.

The following is a list of delicious Whole Foods that are unprocessed or minimally processed that you can enjoy without guilt during your 30 day challenge. Every recipe in this book is fully compliant with these rules and they can all be enjoyed throughout your 30 day challenge and beyond!

- *Poultry and meat:* chicken, duck, turkey, pork, beef, veal, etc.
- *Fish and seafood:* shrimp, crab, scallops, salmon, whitefish, etc.
- *Vegetables:* all vegetables are allowed
- *Fruits:* both fresh and dried fruits are allowed
- *Nuts and seeds:* all nuts and seeds are allowed except peanuts (despite their name, peanuts are in fact legumes, not nuts); nut milks, and flours, are allowed as well. You need to check the ingredients carefully when purchasing these items however, as many commercially produced nut products such as almond milk will also include sugar, which is not allowed.
- *Fats:* ghee (clarified butter), lard, duck fat, coconut oil, healthy plant oils such as olive oil, avocado oil, sesame oil, etc.
- *Herbs and spices:* no restrictions
- *Pantry:* almond flour, coconut flour, red wine vinegar, rice vinegar, apple cider vinegar, balsamic vinegar, beef broth, chicken broth, mustard, pickles, etc.
- *Drinks:* coconut water, fruit juice, kombucha, mineral water, tea, vegetable juice, etc.

On the other hand, the program has its list of foods that are not allowed such as:

- *Alcohol:* no alcohol in any form is allowed
- *Sugar and sweeteners:* sugar of any kind is not allowed
- *Grains:* all grains are to be avoided – rice, oats, corn, buckwheat, quinoa, amaranth, millet, bulgur, etc.
- *Dairy, soy, and soy products*
- *Pulses and legumes:* the exceptions are snow peas, sugar snap peas, and green beans
- *Processed additives:* any food including MSG, carrageenan, or sulfites is to be avoided

How does a slow cooker fit in here?

Slow cookers are a supremely convenient appliance to have in your kitchen for cooking food in a way that is tasty, juicy, and most importantly, healthy. This is especially true when it comes to cooking meat. There is an increasing body of evidence that certain methods of cooking meat, especially methods that involve high heat or an open flame, are linked to some very serious health consequences such as an increased risk of cancer. When you cook with your slow cooker, the meat is simmered over low heat so that harmful compounds can't form while the meat simmers. The flavors of all the ingredients, whether vegetables, meat, or herbs and spices all mingle together creating a finished dish that is bursting with flavor in a way that other cooking methods just can't achieve. Moreover, low temperature cooking allows minerals and vitamins to be preserved and consumed when you eat the food, instead of being destroyed the way they often are with other cooking methods.

Not only is the slow cooker one of the healthiest ways to prepare meals, but it also eliminates the single most common reason people have for not enjoying healthy home cooked meals: lack of time. Not having the time to cook delicious and healthy meals at home is not just an excuse. It is a reality for most of us. Technology, work, and society are changing in ways that have made us all busier than ever before. Finding the time to prepare healthy meals at home can seem like a luxury that is out of reach for so many people. This is tragic, but it doesn't have to be this way. The slow cooker is the one appliance above all others that makes healthy home-cooking accessible for anyone, regardless of how little time, money, or skill you may have in the kitchen. When you combine honest and healthy Whole Food ingredients with your simple and easy slow cooker, what you get is a sustainable way to enjoy eating amazing, healthy meals *for life*.

VEGETARIAN

RECIPES

Sarson ka Saag

IMAGE SOURCE: Pixabay

Servings: 4, Calories: 50.3, Total Fat: 3.9 g, Saturated Fat: 0.1 g, Carbs: 2.2 g, Sugar: 0.3 g, Protein: 0.9 g

Ingredients:
1 red onion, finely chopped

2 Tbsp ghee
2 Tbsp minced garlic
1-2 Serrano peppers, minced
2-inch ginger, minced
½ tsp chili powder
½ tsp turmeric powder
1 tsp cumin powder
1 tsp coriander powder
2 tsp salt
½ tsp black pepper
1 lb fresh baby spinach
1 lb mustard leaves, stem removed, leaves chopped
1 tsp garam masala
1 Tbsp ghee
1 pinch fenugreek leaves

Instructions:

- Add the onion, ghee, garlic, Serrano pepper, ginger, and the spices to your slow cooker. Set on high and cook for an hour.
- In the meantime, add the spinach and mustard to a large pot and fill it with water. Cook on high and when it begins to boil, cook uncovered for about 5 minutes. Drain and set aside to cool.
- Transfer to your blender and blend for a few seconds or until you get the desired consistency. If needed, pour in a little water.
- Add the mixture to the slow cooker, cover and cook on low for 2 hours.
- Add the garam masala, ghee, and fenugreek leaves, give it a good stir, cover and cook on low for one more hour. Serve warm.

Butternut Squash & Apple Soup

IMAGE SOURCE: Pixabay

Servings: 4, Calories: 229.5, Total Fat: 9.6 g, Saturated Fat: 8.4 g, Carbs: 37.8 g, Sugar: 11.4 g, Protein: 2.7 g

Ingredients:
1 medium butternut squash, peeled, seeded, and diced
1/2 yellow onion, peeled and minced
2 large apples
2 Tbsp coconut oil
4 cups water
2 bay leaves
1 tsp ground cinnamon
2 tsp sea salt

1/2 tsp ground black pepper
1 can coconut milk

Instructions:

- Add the ingredients (except the coconut milk) to your slow cooker, mix well, cover and cook on high for 3 to 4 hours or on low for 7 to 8 hours.
- Discard the cinnamon sticks and bay leaves and leave the soup to cool a bit.
- Puree the veggies using an immersion blender until smooth.
- Add the coconut milk and puree for a couple of more minutes to combine.
- Taste, season with salt and pepper and serve warm.

Minestrone Soup

IMAGE SOURCE: Pixabay

Servings: 8, Calories: 99.0, Total Fat: 3.7 g, Saturated Fat: 0.5 g, Carbs: 16.0 g, Sugar: 1.5 g, Protein: 1.9 g

Ingredients:
2 Tbsp olive oil
1 cup carrots, diced
1 yellow sweet potato, diced
2 zucchinis, diced
2 celery stalks, diced
2 cloves garlic, minced
2 shallots, diced
3.5 cup water
1 cup fresh spinach, chopped
1 can (28 oz) diced tomatoes with juices
1 tsp chopped parsley
2 tsp dried oregano
1/4 tsp cayenne pepper
1/4 tsp salt
2 bay leaves

Instructions:

- Add the olive oil to your slow cooker along with the carrots, sweet potato, zucchini, celery, garlic, and shallots.
- Pour in the water, add the spinach, tomatoes, and sprinkle with the parsley, oregano, cayenne, and salt.
- Give it a good stir, add the bay leaves, cover and cook on low for 6-8 hours.
- Once done, discard the bay leaves and serve warm in serving bowls.

Sweet Potato, Apple & Turmeric Soup

Servings: 8, Calories: 290.6, Total Fat: 4.7 g, Saturated Fat: 1.2 g, Carbs: 59.8 g, Sugar: 10.6 g, Protein: 5.2 g

Ingredients:
3 garlic cloves, peeled and smashed
1 medium yellow onion, cut into medium chunks
½ lb russet potatoes, cut into medium chunks
2 lb sweet potatoes, cut into medium chunks
1 lb apples, cored and cut into medium chunks
4 cup water
1 tsp turmeric
1-3 tsp kosher salt
1 cup coconut milk
1 Tbsp apple cider vinegar
Black pepper, for serving

Instructions:

- Add the garlic, onion, russet potatoes, sweet potatoes, apples, and water to your slow cooker. Sprinkle with the turmeric and salt and give it a good stir.
- Cover and cook on low for 5-6 hours or on high for 3-4 hours.
- Once done, uncover and add the coconut milk and apple cider vinegar. Puree the vegetables with an immersion blender until smooth.
- Sprinkle with black pepper and serve warm in serving bowls.

Garlic & Herb Cauliflower Mash

IMAGE SOURCE: Pixabay

Servings: 8, Calories: 31.5, Total Fat: 0.2 g, Saturated Fat: 0.0 g, Carbs: 6.6 g, Sugar: 0.3 g, Protein: 2.2 g

Ingredients:
1 large head cauliflower, cut into florets
1 cup vegetable broth
6 cloves garlic, peeled
4-6 cups water

3 Tbsp ghee
4 Tbsp minced herbs
Salt, to taste

Instructions:

- Place the cauliflower florets into your slow cooker.
- Pour in the broth, add the garlic and enough water to cover the cauliflower.
- Cover and cook on high for 3 hours or on low for 6 hours.
- Once done, drain, discard the liquid and return the cauliflower to the cooker.
- Add the ghee and use and immersion blender to puree the cauliflower.
- Sprinkle with the herbs, season with salt and mix.
- Serve warm.

Anti-Inflammatory Soup

IMAGE SOURCE: Pixabay

Servings: 2, Calories: 94.7, Total Fat: 0.9 g, Saturated Fat: 0.1 g, Carbs: 21.6 g, Sugar: 4.7 g, Protein: 3.1 g

Ingredients:
1 small yellow onion
1/2 cup diced celery
2 1/2 cup diced tomatoes
3/4 cup diced carrots

3 cups water
1/2 tsp dried oregano
1 Tbsp dried basil
1 Tbsp turmeric
1 tsp salt
1/2 tsp black pepper
1 can coconut milk

Instructions:

- Add the ingredients except the coconut milk to your slow cooker. Give it a good stir, cover and cook on low for 6 hours or on high for 4 hours.
- When the cooking time is up, allow the veggies to cool for a few minutes.
- Puree with an immersion blender until smooth.
- Add the coconut milk, stir again to combine and serve.

Cabbage Casserole promeni sliku

IMAGE SOURCE: Pixabay

Servings: 2, Calories: 127.5, Total Fat: 1.3 g, Saturated Fat: 0.2 g, Carbs: 27.4 g, Sugar: 0.2 g, Protein: 7.6 g

Ingredients:
½ cabbage, roughly sliced
3 cloves garlic, minced

1 onion, diced
1.5 cup crushed tomatoes
2 cup prepared cauliflower rice
4 Tbsp ghee
½ tsp crushed red pepper
Salt, to taste
Black pepper, to taste
½ cup finely chopped fresh parsley

Instructions:

- Add all the ingredients except the parsley to your slow cooker. Mix everything well.
- Cover and cook on high for 3-4 hours or on low for 7-8 hours.
- Once cooked, sprinkle with the parsley, stir and serve warm.

Vegetable Korma

IMAGE SOURCE: Pixabay

Servings: 4, Calories: 134.0, Total Fat: 2.5 g, Saturated Fat: 1.4 g, Carbs: 24.2 g, Sugar: 4.2 g, Protein: 7.0 g

Ingredients:
2 large carrots, chopped
1 large cauliflower, cut into florets
1 cup green beans, chopped
1/2 cup frozen green peas

2 cloves garlic, minced
1/2 large onion, chopped
2 Tbsp curry powder
3/4 can coconut milk
1 tsp garam masala
1 tsp sea salt
2 Tbsp almond flour

Instructions:

- Add the carrots, cauliflower, green beans, green peas, garlic, and onion to your slow cooker and give it a good stir.
- In a bowl, combine the curry powder, coconut milk, garam masala, and salt. Pour into the slow cooker, add the almond flour and mix well.
- Cover and cook on high for 5 hours and on low for 8 hours.
- Serve warm.

Chunky Vegetable Soup

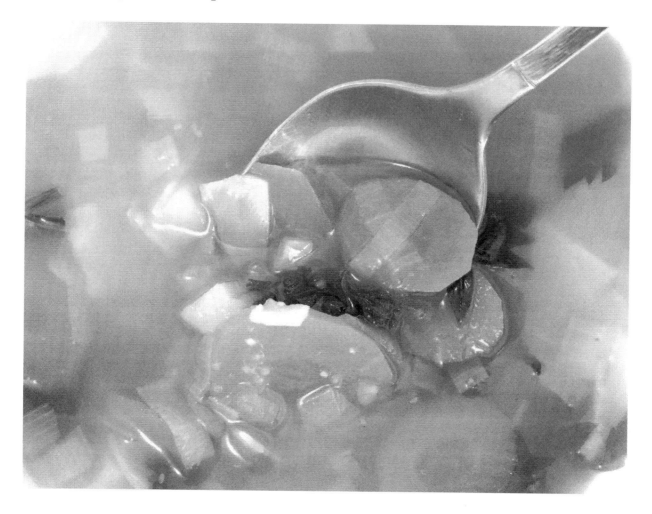

IMAGE SOURCE: Pixabay

Servings: 4, Calories: 111.2, Total Fat: 0.8 g, Saturated Fat: 0.1 g, Carbs: 25.4 g, Sugar: 3.9 g, Protein: 3.4 g

Ingredients:
4 cup water
1 sweet onion, diced

3 cloves garlic, minced
3 celery stalks, chopped
1 bell pepper, chopped
4 carrots, chopped
1 sweet potato, peeled and chopped
3 cups diced tomatoes
1 cup green beans, halved
2 Tbsp dried parsley
1 bay leaf
Salt, to taste

Instructions:

- Add the ingredients to your slow cooker and stir well to combine.
- Cover and cook on high for 3-5 hours.
- Once the vegetables are cooked through, remove the lid and serve warm.

Butternut Squash & Apple Cream Soup

IMAGE SOURCE: Pixabay

Servings: 4, Calories: 202.9, Total Fat: 1.8 g, Saturated Fat: 1.3 g, Carbs: 49.1 g, Sugar: 10.1 g, Protein: 3.8 g

Ingredients:
2 medium apples, peeled, cored, and chopped
6 cup chopped butternut squash
1 garlic clove, chopped
1 small white onion, chopped

2 medium carrots, peeled and chopped
2 cups water
1 1/2 tsp dried thyme
1/2 tsp dried sage
1/2 tsp sea salt
1/4 tsp ground black pepper
1 cup coconut milk
Chopped fresh parsley, for garnish

Instructions:

- Add the apples, squash, garlic, onions, carrots, and water to your slow cooker. Mix in the seasonings and cook on low for 6-8 hours.
- Once the cooking time is up, remove the lid, add the coconut milk and stir well.
- Use an immersion blender to puree the vegetables.
- Season with salt and pepper, garnish with parsley and serve.

Curried Kale & Green Beans

IMAGE SOURCE: Pixabay

Servings: 2, Calories: 181.6, Total Fat: 5.8 g, Saturated Fat: 5.1 g, Carbs: 27.9 g, Sugar: 12.4 g, Protein: 5.7 g

Ingredients:

1 medium head of kale, rinsed and roughly chopped
2 handful of raw green beans, ends trimmed
1 can coconut milk
4 cups vegetable broth
1 Tbsp curry powder

Instructions:

- Pour the broth and coconut milk into your slow cooker. Add the curry powder and stir well.
- Add the kale and green beans and stir to coat the greens with the liquid.
- Cook on low for 4-5 hours or on high for 2-3 hours.
- Once done, serve warm.

Butternut Squash Soup

IMAGE SOURCE: Pixabay

Servings: 6, Calories: 64.0, Total Fat: 0.2 g, Saturated Fat: 0.0 g, Carbs: 16.0 g, Sugar: 1.7 g, Protein: 1.5 g

Ingredients:
1 butternut squash, peeled, deseeded, and chopped
3 carrots, peeled and chopped
1 onion, chopped
3 garlic cloves, minced

4 cups water
Salt, to taste
Black pepper, to taste

Instructions:

- Add the ingredients to your slow cooker.
- Cover and cook on low for about 6-8 hours.
- Once done, puree the veggies with an immersion blender.
- Season with salt and pepper and serve.

Rustic Tomato Soup

IMAGE SOURCE: Pixabay

Servings: 8, Calories: 121.8, Total Fat: 4.6 g, Saturated Fat: 0.9 g, Carbs: 24.1 g, Sugar: 7.6 g, Protein: 4.4 g

Ingredients:
2 celery stalks, chopped
2 carrots, peeled and chopped
4 garlic cloves, minced
1 onion, chopped
1 can (14 oz) roasted red peppers with juices
72 oz can whole tomatoes with juices
1/4 cup fresh basil
4 cups water
1 bay leaf
Salt, to taste
Black pepper, to taste

Instructions:

- Add the ingredients to your slow cooker.
- Cook on low for 8 hours.
- Once the cooking time is up, use an immersion blender to blend the vegetables until smooth.
- Taste, season with salt and pepper and serve.

Balsamic Root Veggies

IMAGE SOURCE: Pexels

Servings: 6, Calories: 176.7, Total Fat: 0.7 g, Saturated Fat: 0.1 g, Carbs: 41.3 g, Sugar: 12.4 g, Protein: 3.8 g

Ingredients:
1 lb parsnips, chopped
1 lb sweet potatoes, chopped
1 lb carrots, chopped
1 rutabaga, peeled and chopped

4 cloves garlic, minced
1 onion, chopped
1/4 cup water
1/4 cup balsamic vinegar
1 Tbsp olive oil
1/4 cup unsweetened apple juice
Salt, to taste
Black pepper, to taste

Instructions:

- Add all the ingredients to your slow cooker.
- Set on low and cook for 6-8 hours. Check a couple of times, and if it dry, add more water.
- Serve warm.

Creamy Pumpkin Soup

IMAGE SOURCE: Pixabay

Servings: 8, Calories: 154.6, Total Fat: 5.1 g, Saturated Fat: 1.7 g, Carbs: 25.0 g, Sugar: 18.2 g, Protein: 1.7 g

Ingredients:
2 Tbsp olive oil
4 large carrots, peeled and diced
1 large yellow onion, diced
2 celery stalks, diced
1 Tbsp curry powder

4 cloves garlic, finely minced

1 tsp ground cumin

1/4 tsp cayenne pepper

1 tsp ground coriander

1/8 tsp ground nutmeg

Salt, to taste

Black pepper, to taste

1 can (14 oz) coconut milk

6 cups vegetable broth

20 oz pumpkin puree

1/4 cup chopped cilantro, for garnish

1/4 cup pumpkin seeds, for garnish

Instructions:

- Heat the oil in a pan on medium. Add the carrots, onion, and celery and sauté for 10 minutes.
- Once tender, stir in the curry powder, garlic, cumin, cayenne, coriander, and nutmeg and season with salt and pepper.
- Cook for 2-3 more minutes, stirring continuously, and transfer the sautéed veggies to you're a slow cooker.
- Pour in the coconut milk, broth and mix in the pumpkin puree. Cover and cook on high for 4 hours or on low for 8 hours.
- Once cooked, use and immersion blender and puree until smooth.
- Garnish with the cilantro and pumpkin seeds and serve.

CHICKEN RECIPES

Peach BBQ Chicken

IMAGE SOURCE: Pixabay

Servings: 8, Calories: 218.0, Total Fat: 3.9 g, Saturated Fat: 0.9 g, Carbs: 15.4 g, Sugar: 8.8 g, Protein: 30.7 g

Ingredients for the peach sauce:
4 dates, pitted
½ cup boiling water
2 Tbsp ghee
½ cup minced onion
3 cloves garlic, minced

2 medium peaches, peeled and roughly chopped
1 can (12 oz) tomato sauce
1 can (6 oz) tomato paste
¼ cup mustard
¼ cup apple cider vinegar
1 Tbsp chili powder
1 tsp smoked paprika
1 pinch ground cloves
¼ tsp ground cumin
Sea salt, to taste
Black pepper, to taste

Ingredients for the chicken:
2 lb boneless chicken breasts, skin removed
1 cup peach sauce

Ingredients for the slaw:
2 cups shredded cabbage
2 Tbsp apple cider vinegar
2 Tbsp avocado oil
Sea salt, to taste
Black pepper, to taste

Instructions:

To prepare the sauce:
- Add the dates to a blender, pour in the boiling water, cover and set aside for 5 minutes.
- In the meantime, melt the ghee in a saucepan on medium. Add the onions and sauté for about 5-7 minutes.
- Once softened, add the garlic and cook for half a minute or until fragrant.
- Transfer the sautéed garlic and onion to the dates along with the remaining sauce ingredients.
- Blend until smooth and season with salt and pepper. Reserve 1 cup and store the rest in a glass jar. It will keep for up to 2 weeks in the fridge.
  To prepare the chicken:
- Add the chicken to your slow cooker. Pour the reserved sauce and stir to coat.
- Cover and cook on low for about 5-6 hours.
- Once the cooking time is up, leave the chicken to cool, leaving it in the cooker.
- Shred, toss and transfer to a serving dish.

- To prepare the slow:
- Mix the ingredients in a bowl and serve with the chicken.

Chicken Pho With Vegetable Noodles

IMAGE SOURCE: Pixabay

Servings: 6, Calories: 137.1, Total Fat: 3.0 g, Saturated Fat: 1.7 g, Carbs: 6.7 g, Sugar: 2.8 g, Protein: 21.1 g

Ingredients:
1 lb boneless chicken breasts, skin removed
8 cups chicken broth
2-inch ginger, sliced
1 white onion, sliced

3 garlic cloves, smashed
1/2 tsp white pepper
1 dash of cinnamon
2 medium zucchinis, spiralized

Instructions:

- Add the ingredients except the noodles to your slow cooker.
- Cover and cook on low for about 5-6 hours.
- Strain the soup discarding the onion, garlic, and ginger.
- Shred the chicken and divide the soup between the serving bowls.
- Add the zucchini noodles and serve.

White Chicken Chili

IMAGE SOURCE: Pixabay

Servings: 6, Calories: 237.0, Total Fat: 4.2 g, Saturated Fat: 1.7 g, Carbs: 15.9 g, Sugar: 2.6 g, Protein: 32.2 g

Ingredients:
1.5 lb boneless chicken breasts, skin removed
2 cups chicken broth

3 cups chopped potato

1 Tbsp finely chopped jalapeños

4 oz canned diced green chilies

4 cloves garlic, finely chopped

1 yellow onion, diced

1 tsp dried cilantro

⅛ tsp cayenne pepper

½ tsp chili powder

1 tsp oregano

2 tsp cumin

1 tsp salt

¼ tsp black pepper

½ cup coconut milk

1 Tbsp organic ghee

1 Tbsp fresh lime juice

Instructions:

- Place the chicken in your slow cooker and add the broth, potatoes, jalapeno, green chilies, garlic, onion, and spices, and season with salt and pepper.
- Cook on low for 6 to 7 hours or on high for 3 to 4 hours.
- Once done, transfer the chicken to a dish or plate, leaving the vegetables in the cooker.
- Add the remaining ingredients to the cooker and give it a good stir and cook covered on high for 20 more minutes.
- Meanwhile, shred the chicken and after 20 minutes are up, add it back to the cooker. Cover again and cook on high for 10 more minutes.
- When the cooking time is up, allow to cool for a couple of minutes and serve

Farmer's Chicken Soup

IMAGE SOURCE: Pixabay

Servings: 4, Calories: 95.9, Total Fat: 1.1 g, Saturated Fat: 0.9 g, Carbs: 19.0 g, Sugar: 8.8 g, Protein: 4.9 g

Ingredients:
2 lb boneless chicken breasts, skin removed
1 can (15 oz) tomato sauce
4 cups chicken broth
4 cups water
1 yellow onion, finely chopped
1 tsp garlic powder
1 tsp cumin
½ tsp chili powder
2-3 tsp salt
3 cups chopped kale leaves
3 medium zucchinis, chopped
2 limes, juiced
16 oz cherry tomatoes, halved

Instructions:

- Add the chicken to your slow cooker along with the tomato sauce, broth, water, onion, garlic powder, cumin, chili powder, and salt.
- Cook covered on low for 6 hours or on high for 4 hours.
- Once the cooking time is over, remove the chicken, shred it and put it back to the cooker.
- Add the greens and zucchini.
- Cook covered for half an hour.
- Once the zucchini is tender, squeeze in the lime juice, stir, top with the tomatoes and serve.

Chicken Sloppy Joe

IMAGE SOURCE: Pixabay

30 DAY WHOLE FOOD SLOW COOKER CHALLENGE

Servings: 8, Calories: 131.3, Total Fat: 1.4 g, Saturated Fat: 0.3 g, Carbs: 20.4 g, Sugar: 8.3 g, Protein: 10.9 g

Ingredients:
1 lb boneless chicken thighs, skin removed
1 lb boneless chicken breasts, skin removed
¼ cup canned tomato paste
1 can (14 oz) can tomato sauce
¾ cup shredded carrots
3 dates, finely chopped
2 Tbsp apple cider vinegar
3 Tbsp mustard
½ tsp onion powder
1 tsp garlic powder
½ tsp chili powder
¼ tsp sea salt
¼ tsp black pepper
2 sweet potatoes, sliced into thin rounds
Avocado oil

Instructions:

- Add the ingredients to your slow cooker, mix to combine and cook covered on low for about 4-6 hours.
- Once the cooking time is up, remove the chicken from the cooker, shred it and return back to the cooker.
- While the chicken is cooking, roast the potatoes.
- Preheat the oven to 375F / 190C.
- Brush the potato rounds with olive oil and season with salt. Bake in the preheated oven for about 15 minutes.
- Once baked, remove from the oven and leave to cool slightly.
- Serve the chicken on half the potato rounds and top with the remaining rounds (or serve on cauliflower rice if preferred)

Green Chile Chicken

IMAGE SOURCE: Pixabay

Servings: 6, Calories: 71.9, Total Fat: 2.1 g, Saturated Fat: 0.5 g, Carbs: 3.6 g, Sugar: 0.9 g, Protein: 9.6 g

Ingredients:
2.5- 3 lb boneless, chicken thighs, skin removed
1 tsp ground coriander
2 tsp cumin

1.5 tsp sea salt
1 tsp black pepper
1 medium onion, diced
3-4 tomatillos, husked and diced
3 cloves garlic, finely chopped
1/2 lb Hatch chiles, diced
Lime wedges, for garnish
Chopped cilantro, for garnish

Instructions:

- Add the chicken to your slow cooker and sprinkle with coriander, cumin, salt, and black pepper.
- Toss to combine and add the onion, tomatillos, garlic, and green chilies.
- Seal the lid and cook on low for 5 hours.
- Once done, shred the chicken, stir well to combine and serve warm.

Butter Chicken

IMAGE SOURCE: Pixabay

Servings: 4, Calories: 584.0, Total Fat: 21.6 g, Saturated Fat: 9.9 g, Carbs: 18.0 g, Sugar: 10.9 g, Protein: 76.8 g

Ingredients:
1 Tbsp coconut oil
1 onion, diced
3-4 cloves garlic, crushed

3/4 cup tomato paste

1 3/4 cups coconut milk

2 Tbsp garam masala

2 Tbsp tapioca starch

1 tsp curry powder

1/2 tsp chili powder

1/2 tsp ginger powder

Salt, to taste

Black pepper, to taste

2.7 lb chicken thighs, cut into bite-size pieces

Instructions:

- Add the coconut oil to a pan and heat on medium. Add the garlic and onion and sauté for a few minutes.
- Once translucent, stir in the remaining ingredients, except the chicken.
- Cook, stirring frequently until the sauce has thickened. Season with salt and pepper, stir and set aside.
- Add the chicken to your slow cooker, pour in the sauce and mix well.
- Seal the lid and cook on low for 5 hours.
- Once the cooking time is up, allow to cool for a few minutes and serve.

Chicken, Kale & Sweet Potato Stew

IMAGE SOURCE: Pixabay

Servings: 6, Calories: 176.3, Total Fat: 2.6 g, Saturated Fat: 0.6 g, Carbs: 17.1 g, Sugar: 4.6 g, Protein: 21.3 g

Ingredients:
1 lb chicken breasts, skin removed, cut into chunks
3 carrots, peeled and cubed
1 yellow onion, diced

3 garlic cloves, minced
1 sweet potato, peeled and cubed
1 cup water
1/3 cup tomato paste
2 tsp mustard
3 Tbsp balsamic vinegar
3 bay leaves
1 bunch of kale, stems removed, leaves torn up
Salt, to taste
Fresh pepper, to taste

Instructions:

- Add the chicken to your slow cooker. Top with the carrots, onions, garlic, and sweet potato. Pour in the water and add the tomato paste, mustard, balsamic vinegar, and bay leaves and stir to combine.
- Cook on high for 4-5 hours. In the last hour of cooking, add the kale, season with salt and pepper and mix well.
- Once done, shred the chicken or leave it in chunks, discard the bay leaves and serve.

Lemony Chicken & Kale Soup

IMAGE SOURCE: Pixabay

Servings: 6, Calories: 330.1, Total Fat: 22.0 g, Saturated Fat: 3.5 g, Carbs: 6.8 g, Sugar: 1.1 g, Protein: 26.5 g

Ingredients:
6 cups water, divided use
1/2 cup olive oil
1 cup chopped onions

4 cups shredded chicken
1 bunch of kale, sliced into strips
2 Tbsp fresh lemon juice
Zest of 3 lemons
Salt, to taste

Instructions:

- Pour 2 cups of water to a blender along with the olive oil and onion and blend until smooth.
- Pour the mixture into a slow cooker along with the remaining water. Add the chicken, kale, lemon juice and zest and season with salt.
- Cook on low for 6 hours, checking and stirring a couple of times during cooking.
- Serve warm.

Chicken Cacciatore

IMAGE SOURCE: Pixabay

Servings: 6, Calories: 261.5, Total Fat: 5.1 g, Saturated Fat: 1.3 g, Carbs: 12.1 g, Sugar: 3.3 g, Protein: 42.2 g

Ingredients:
1 onion, thinly sliced
4 garlic cloves, sliced
2 celery stalks with leaves, diced
1 green pepper, chopped

1 lb mushrooms, sliced

1 can (14 oz) diced tomatoes

1/2 cup chicken broth

4 Tbsp tomato paste

1 1/2 Tbsp capers, drained

1/2 tsp red pepper flakes

2 lb boneless chicken breast, skin removed, roughly chopped

Instructions:

- Add the ingredients except the chicken to your slow cooker and give them a good stir.
- Season the chicken with salt and pepper and add it to the cooker.
- Set on low and cook for 4-6 hours.
- Serve warm.

Chicken Tikka Masala

IMAGE SOURCE: Pixabay

Servings: 4, Calories: 240.9, Total Fat: 6.2 g, Saturated Fat: 1.8 g, Carbs: 16.6 g, Sugar: 4.9 g, Protein: 30.5 g

Ingredients:
2 Tbsp ghee
6 garlic cloves, minced
1 onion, chopped
1 tsp garam masala
8 boneless chicken thighs, skin removed

1 lemon, juiced
1 tsp salt
1 can (5-6 oz) tomato paste
1 can (15 oz) diced tomatoes, drained
Cayenne pepper, to taste
1 small bunch cilantro, minced
1/4 cup unsweetened coconut milk

Instructions:

- Add the ghee, garlic, onion, and garam masala to a bowl and microwave for 5 minutes, stirring a couple of times. When done, mix in the tomato paste and set aside.
- Add the chicken to your slow cooker, drizzle with the lemon juice and season with salt.
- Pour over the onion mixture, add the diced tomatoes and sprinkle with cayenne. Mix well to coat the chicken.
- Cover and cook on low for 4-6 hours.
- Once done, add the cilantro and coconut milk, stir well and serve.

Nourishing Chicken Soup

IMAGE SOURCE: Pixabay

Servings: 8, Calories: 199.5, Total Fat: 5.5 g, Saturated Fat: 1.8 g, Carbs: 10.7 g, Sugar: 4.5 g, Protein: 26.7 g

Ingredients:
2 lb chicken thighs bone-in, skin removed
2 thyme sprigs
2 cloves garlic, minced
5 cups chicken broth
1 lb carrots, peeled, sliced lengthwise
1 yellow onion, diced
1/2 Tbsp chopped fresh thyme
1/2 bunch kale, stems removed, leaves chopped
Salt, to taste

Black pepper, to taste

Instructions:

- Add the chicken to your crock pot, season with salt and pepper and add the thyme sprigs and garlic.
- Pour in the broth, cover and cook on high for 4 hours.
- Take the chicken out of the cooker, discard the thyme sprigs, strain the cooking liquid and pour it back into the cooker.
- Shred the chicken and keep it in the fridge; put the bones back to the cooker. Add the onions, carrot and fresh thyme and cook on high for 1.5 hours.
- Add the kale and cook for 30 more minutes. Discard the chicken bones, taste and season with salt and pepper if needed.
- Put the chicken back to the cooker, reheat for about 10 minutes and serve warm.

Chipotle Chicken Soup

IMAGE SOURCE: Pixabay

Servings: 4, Calories: 190.9, Total Fat: 7.3 g, Saturated Fat: 2.1 g, Carbs: 14.9 g, Sugar: 3.2 g, Protein: 18.1 g

Ingredients:
2 carrots, sliced
1 purple onion, peeled and chopped
4 cloves garlic, minced
2 celery stalk, chopped

2 chipotle chilies, chopped

1 can petite diced tomatoes

1 cup diced yellow summer squash

1 Tbsp olive oil

20 oz boneless chicken thighs, skin removed, fat trimmed

4 cups chicken broth

1 tsp ground cumin

2 tsp salt

1/2 cup chopped fresh cilantro leaves

1 lime, quartered

Instructions:

- Add the carrots, onion, garlic, celery, and chilies to your slow cooker. Stir well and add the tomatoes and squash.
- Heat the oil in a pan on medium. Add the chicken and fry for 2-3 minutes per side. Once lightly browned, put the chicken into the cooker.
- Pour the broth into the pan, heat and scrape the browned bits and pour into the slow cooker.
- Season with the cumin and salt and cook covered on high for 3-4 hours or on low for 6-7 hours.
- Once the cooking time is up, take the chicken out, shred and return to the cooker. Give it a gentle stir to combine, garnish with the cilantro and lime and serve.

Butternut Chicken With Pears & Cranberries

IMAGE SOURCE: Pexels

Servings: 4, Calories: 362.8, Total Fat: 5.8 g, Saturated Fat: 1.6 g, Carbs: 31.3 g, Sugar: 5.2 g, Protein: 47.7 g

Ingredients:
1 butternut squash, cubed
1 bosc pear, sliced
1 sweet onion, sliced
1 cup raw cranberries
1.5 lb boneless, chicken breasts, skin removed, quartered
2 bay leaves

2 tsp cinnamon

2 tsp garlic powder

1 tsp sea salt

1 tsp black pepper

1 cup chicken broth

Instructions:

- Add the squash to your slow cooker, half the pears, onions, and cranberries.
- Tuck in 1 bay leaf and sprinkle with half the cinnamon, garlic powder, salt, and pepper.
- Add the chicken into one layer and then top with the remaining pears, onion, and cranberries.
- Tuck in another bay leaf and sprinkle with the remaining spices.
- Pour in the broth, cover and cook on low for 6-8 hours.
- Serve warm.

Brazilian-Style Chicken

IMAGE SOURCE: Pixabay

Servings: 4, Calories: 306.2, Total Fat: 7.4 g, Saturated Fat: 2.7 g, Carbs: 11.3 g, Sugar: 4.4 g, Protein: 47.6 g

Ingredients:
2 Tbsp tomato paste
¾ cup coconut milk
1 Tbsp ground ginger
3 garlic cloves, minced
4-6 Tbsp curry powder
1 yellow onion, thinly sliced
2 bell peppers, diced
1.5-2 lb chicken breasts
1 cup chicken broth
Salt, to taste
Black pepper, to taste

Instructions:

- Add the tomato paste, coconut milk, ginger, garlic, and curry powder to your slow cooker. Season with salt and pepper and stir well.
- Add the onions, peppers, and chicken and pour in the broth.
- Stir well to coat the chicken with the mixture, cover and cook on high for 4-5 hours or on low for 6-8 hours.
- Serve warm.

PORK RECIPES

Crispy Carnitas

IMAGE SOURCE: Pixabay

Servings: 6, Calories: 319.6, Total Fat: 10.2 g, Saturated Fat: 4.0 g, Carbs: 9.0 g, Sugar: 4.3 g, Protein: 48.9 g

Ingredients:
3 lb pork loin roast
2 tsp oregano
½ tsp chili powder

1 tsp cumin powder
Salt, to taste
Black pepper, to taste
6 cloves garlic, minced
1 onion, coarsely chopped
1 bay leaf
1-2 Serrano peppers, minced
1 cinnamon stick
1 lime, juice
2 oranges, juiced
3 Tbsp ghee

Instructions:

- Rinse the pork and put it into your slow cooker. Season both sides with oregano, chili powder, cumin, salt, and pepper.
- Add the garlic, onion, bay leaf, Serrano pepper, and cinnamon stick.
- Squeeze in the lime and oranges, cover and cook on low for 6 to 8 hours or on high for 4 hours.
- Once done, use two forks to shred the pork. Do not discard the liquid.
- Add the ghee to a skillet and when melted, add the shredded meat and fry until crispy and golden.
- Arrange on a plate, drizzle with the cooking liquid and lime juice and serve warm.

Cantonese Ham & Lotus Root Soup

IMAGE SOURCE: Pixabay

Servings: 4, Calories: 83.5, Total Fat: 5.1 g, Saturated Fat: 1.8 g, Carbs: 4.7 g, Sugar: 0.0 g, Protein: 5.1 g

Ingredients:
2 small lotus roots, peeled and cut into ¼ inch thick slices

8-10 cups water
1 ham bone with some meat left on it

Instructions:

- Place the lotus root slices into a bowl, fill it with water and leave to soak for several minutes. Rinse and add to the slow cooker.
- Add the water and ham bone, cover and cook on low for 6 hours.
- When the cooking time is over, take out the bone, remove the meat off the bone and put the bone and meat back to the slow cooker.
- Cover and cook on low for 2 more hours.
- Once done, discard the bone and serve warm.

Chili Verde

IMAGE SOURCE: Pexels

Servings: 8, Calories: 201.0, Total Fat: 12.0 g, Saturated Fat: 2.3 g, Carbs: 2.7 g, Sugar: 0.2 g, Protein: 19.5 g

Ingredients:
2 cups beef broth
1/4 cup olive oil
1 Tbsp dried cilantro
1/2 tsp oregano
1 tsp cumin
2 tsp sea salt
1/2 tsp black pepper
3/4 lb chiles, deseeded, finely diced
2 jalapenos, deseeded and diced
1 medium onion, diced
6 cloves garlic, minced
1 1/2 lbs pork tenderloin, chopped

Instructions:

- Pour the broth into your slow cooker, drizzle in the olive oil and add the spices. Give it a good stir.
- Add the veggies and pork, cover and cook on high for 6 hours.
- Once done, divide between serving bowls and serve warm.

Kalua Pork

IMAGE SOURCE: Pixabay

Servings: 2, Calories: 387.1, Total Fat: 14.4 g, Saturated Fat: 3.7 g, Carbs: 6.8 g, Sugar: 0.0 g, Protein: 53.1 g

Ingredients:
1.5 lb pork shoulder
2-3 Tbsp Hawaiian sea salt
Cauliflower rice, for serving
Wilted cabbage, for serving

Instructions:

- Use a fork to stab at the pork and make puncture, place into a slow cooker and season with salt.
- Seal the lid and cook on low for about 7-12 hours depending on the size of the pork.
- Once cooked, use two forks to shred it.
- Serve with cauliflower rice or with wilted cabbage.

Pork Lettuce Tacos

IMAGE SOURCE: Pixabay

Servings: 6, Calories: 587.8, Total Fat: 27.1 g, Saturated Fat: 8.6 g, Carbs: 13.4 g, Sugar: 5.7 g, Protein: 67.3 g

Ingredients:
1 Tbsp olive oil

4 lb pork chops
1 can (6 oz) tomato paste, unsalted
1 can (14.5 oz) can diced tomatoes
1 cup chicken broth, unsalted
1 lime, juice and zest
1 Tbsp chili powder
1 Tbsp apple cider vinegar
1 tsp cayenne
1 head of lettuce

Instructions:

- Heat the olive oil in a large pan on medium.
- Once hot enough, add the pork chops and fry for about 3-4 minutes per side (work in batches if necessary).
- Once the pork is seared, transfer it to your slow cooker and add the remaining ingredients except the lettuce.
- Cover and cook on low for 8 hours.
- Once done, shred the pork and serve it wrapped in the lettuce leaves.

Smoked Bacon Soup

IMAGE SOURCE: Pixabay

Servings: 6. Calories: 124.3, Total Fat: 3.4 g, Saturated Fat: 1.0 g, Carbs: 18.6 g, Sugar: 4.0 g, Protein: 4.8 g

Ingredients:
3 cups chopped potato
6 cups vegetable broth
2 cups sliced mushrooms
2 cups Brussels sprout shavings

5 pieces smoked bacon, cut into bite-size pieces
1 Tbsp mustard
1 Tbsp olive oil
1/2 tsp paprika
1/4 tsp minced garlic
Salt, to taste
Black pepper, to taste
1 Tbsp dried herbs

Instructions:

- Steam the potatoes for about 90 seconds in a microwave and transfer them to your slow cooker.
- Pour in the broth, add the vegetables, and top with the chopped bacon.
- Add the mustard, oil, paprika, and garlic, season with salt and pepper and stir well.
- Cook on high for 3 hours or on low for about 5-6 hours.
- Once done, allow to cool for a couple of minutes and serve garnished with the herbs.

Slow Cooker Chili

IMAGE SOURCE: Pixabay

Servings: 12, Calories: 471.7, Total Fat: 27.5 g, Saturated Fat: 9.2 g, Carbs: 8.5 g, Sugar: 1.5 g, Protein: 45.7 g

Ingredients:
2 lb pork shoulder, cut into medium chunks
4 lb stew meat, cut into medium chunks
Olive oil, for frying
2.5 lb tomatoes, coarsely chopped, juices reserved

3 Tbsp dark cocoa powder

3 Tbsp smoked paprika

6 cloves garlic, coarsely chopped

2 Tbsp ground cumin

1 tsp sea salt

1 tsp black pepper

2 onions, coarsely chopped

1 lb various fresh chiles, coarsely chopped

Instructions

- Season the pork with salt and pepper and leave to rest for an hour.
- Heat a dash of olive oil in a pan on medium, and working in batches, fry the meat until browned on all sides. Once done, transfer to a plate.
- In a bowl, combine the tomatoes (with the juices), cocoa powder, paprika, garlic, cumin, paprika, salt, and pepper.
- Add the onions to your slow cooker, and then add a layer of chiles, pork, and the tomato mix.
- Cover and cook on low for 9 hours. Remove the lid and cook for 1 more hour.
- Serve warm.

Slow-Cooker Pineapple Pulled Pork

IMAGE SOURCE: Pixabay

Servings: 2, Calories: 1,107.1, Total Fat: 72.9 g, Saturated Fat: 26.4 g, Carbs: 38.0 g, Sugar: 26.7 g, Protein: 72.9 g

Ingredients:
1 small onion, roughly diced
1 ½ lb pork shoulder
½ cup water
½ cup pineapple juice

1 Tbsp mustard

½ cup chopped tomatoes

3 cloves garlic, sliced

2 tsp paprika

½ tsp ground cumin

2 tsp apple cider vinegar

1 cup pineapple, chopped into small chunks

Instructions:

- Add the onion to your slow cooker and top with the pork. Drizzle in the water and juice.
- In a bowl, whisk together the mustard, tomatoes, garlic, paprika, cumin, and vinegar. Once the ingredients are well blended, pour the mixture over the pork.
- Cover and cook on high for 5 hours or on low for 7 hours.
- When the cooking time is up, shred the pork, add the chopped pineapple, mix well and serve.

Mustard Pork Chops With Apples

IMAGE SOURCE: Pixabay

Servings: 6, Calories: 243.7, Total Fat: 9.2 g, Saturated Fat: 3.0 g, Carbs: 14.0 g, Sugar: 9.2 g, Protein: 24.5 g

Ingredients:
1½ lb pork chops
5 small apples, peeled and sliced
1 onion, sliced

1 tsp mustard
1 Tbsp lemon juice
½ tsp salt
Black pepper, to taste

Instructions:

- Add the pork to your slow cooker. Place the onion and apples in a bowl and set aside.
- In a bowl, whisk together the mustard and lemon juice and season with salt and pepper. Drizzle over the onion and apples and toss. Transfer to the slow cooker, cover and cook on high for 5-6 hours or on low for 7-8 hours.
- Serve warm.

Pumpkin & Apple Pork

IMAGE SOURCE: Pixabay

Servings: 4, Calories: 935.1, Total Fat: 47.2 g, Saturated Fat: 13.5 g, Carbs: 19.6 g, Sugar: 9.2 g, Protein: 97.8 g

Ingredients:
3 Tbsp extra virgin olive oil
4 lb bone-in pork chops
1 1/2 large white onions, thinly sliced
2 Tbsp almond flour

1 cup apple cider vinegar
2 apples, peeled and sliced into wedges
1 small pumpkin, peeled and sliced
1/4 tsp nutmeg
Salt, to taste
Black pepper, to taste
8-10 sprigs of fresh thyme

Instructions:

- Heat the olive oil in a pan on medium. Add the pork, season with salt and pepper and cook for about 5 minutes until browned on both sides (work in batches). Transfer to your slow cooker.
- Add the onions to the same pan and sauté for a few minutes or until translucent.
- Stir in the almond flour, cook for a minute, add the vinegar and season with salt and pepper. Cook, stirring frequently, until the sauce thickens. Pour over the pork in the cooker.
- Add the apples and pumpkin, season with the nutmeg and salt and sprinkle with the thyme.
- Cover and cook on low for 8 hours.
- Serve warm and with egg if desired.

BEEF RECIPES

Asian-Style Short Ribs

IMAGE SOURCE: Pixabay

Servings: 4, Calories: 152.2, Total Fat: 8.3 g, Saturated Fat: 1.2 g, Carbs: 19.7 g, Sugar: 7.0 g, Protein: 2.6 g

Ingredients for the ribs:
1/2 yellow onion, roughly chopped
3 celery stalks, roughly chopped
3-4 carrots, roughly chopped
10-15 baby shiitake, sliced
1 lemongrass stalk, sliced and smashed, tough outer layers discarded
1 Tbsp minced garlic
1 tsp finely grated ginger
1-2 Tbsp olive oil

1-2 lbs short ribs
Salt, to taste
Black pepper, to taste
1 large handful snap peas

Ingredients for the sauce:
1/3 cup chicken broth
1 tsp toasted sesame oil
1/4 tsp crushed red chili pepper
1 raw date, diced
1 tsp arrowroot powder

Ingredients for serving:
Cilantro
Sesame seeds

Instructions:

- Add the vegetables except the snap peas, to the slow cooker.
- Generously season the ribs with salt and pepper.
- Heat the olive oil in a pan, add the ribs and fry on high until browned on all sides.
  To prepare the sauce:
- Whisk together the chicken broth, toasted sesame oil, chili flakes, dates, and arrowroot powder. Drizzle the sauce over the vegetables in the slow cooker and stir to coat.
- Add the browned ribs, cover and cook on low for 8-10 hours or on high for 4-5 hours.
- Once done, discard the lemongrass, add the snap peas, mix well, garnish with cilantro and sesame seeds and serve.

Habanero Chili

IMAGE SOURCE: Pixabay

Servings: 4, Calories: 501.4, Total Fat: 37.6 g, Saturated Fat: 14.1 g, Carbs: 18.7 g, Sugar: 3.9 g, Protein: 23.6 g

Ingredients:
1 Tbsp olive oil
4-5 cloves garlic, minced
1 onion, diced
1 lb ground beef

1-2 habaneros, chopped

3 stalks celery, chopped

5 medium carrots, chopped

1 bell pepper, chopped

2 cans (14.5 oz) diced tomatoes

1 ½ tsp cumin powder

2 tsp oregano

1 tsp paprika

1 Tbsp chili powder

1 tsp salt, adjust to taste

Bacon, crumbled, for serving

Instructions:

- Heat the oil in a pan on medium, add the garlic and onions and sauté for a few minutes.
- Once softened, add the ground beef and stir-fry until browned.
- Transfer the ground beef to your slow cooker along with the remaining vegetables, spices, and seasonings.
- Seal the lid and cook on low for 4-5 minutes.
- Once done, transfer to a serving bowl, top with the crumbled bacon and serve warm.

Garlic Roast Beef

IMAGE SOURCE: Pixabay

Servings: 4, Calories: 340.5, Total Fat: 22.0 g, Saturated Fat: 1.6 g, Carbs: 1.0 g, Sugar: 0.0 g, Protein: 32.2 g

Ingredients:
Olive oil, for frying

1 beef roast
4 cloves garlic, sliced
2 Tbsp apple cider vinegar
Salt, to taste
Black pepper, to taste

Instructions:

- Heat a dash of olive oil into a skillet, add the roast and sear on all sides.
- Transfer to a slow cooker and pour in enough water so that the meat is almost submerged in water (the top should not be covered).
- Add the sliced garlic and vinegar and season with salt and pepper.
- Cook on high, and when it begins to bubble, reduce the heat to low. Check when the thermometer reads 150F / 65C.
- Once done, remove from the cooker, slice and serve.

Coconut Milk Curry Beef Stew

IMAGE SOURCE: Pixabay

Servings: 4, Calories: 769.1, Total Fat: 49.1 g, Saturated Fat: 23.4 g, Carbs: 38.9 g, Sugar: 8.7 g, Protein: 43.6 g

Ingredients:
2 Tbsp coconut oil
2 lb stewing beef, roughly chopped
1/4 tsp salt
2 celery stalks, chopped
2 onions, chopped

3 parsnips, chopped
2 carrots, chopped
1 sweet potato, chopped
1 cup coconut milk
3 cups beef broth
1 Tbsp curry powder
Salt, to taste

Instructions:

- Pour the oil in a large pan and heat on medium-high. Add the beef, season with ¼ teaspoon salt and cook until browned. Transfer to your slow cooker.
- In the same pan used for browning the beef, add the celery and onion and sauté for 5 minutes or until lightly browned. Transfer to the slow cooker along with the parsnips, carrots, and sweet potato.
- In a bowl, whisk the coconut milk, broth, and curry powder and pour it over the beef and vegetables in the cooker.
- Cover and cook on high for 4 hours or on low for 8 hours.
- When the cooking time is over, season with salt, and serve warm.

Beef Meatballs In Marinara Sauce

IMAGE SOURCE: Pixabay

Servings: 8, Calories: 413.5, Total Fat: 29.6 g, Saturated Fat: 11.2 g, Carbs: 17.8 g, Sugar: 4.2 g, Protein: 21.8 g

Ingredients for the meatballs:
¼ cup almond flour
½ tsp garlic powder
2 tsp onion powder
¾ tsp salt, divided use
1 pinch red pepper

1 ¾ lb ground beef
1 egg
1 Tbsp chopped fresh parsley

Ingredients for the sauce:
1 can (6 oz) tomato paste
1 can (14 oz) diced tomatoes
1 can (28 oz) crushed tomatoes
½ medium onion, chopped
2 Tbsp chopped oregano leaves
2 Tbsp chopped fresh garlic
2 bay leaves
Salt, to taste

Instructions:

To prepare the meatballs:

- Combine the almond flour, garlic and onion powder, ½ teaspoon salt, and red pepper, and set aside.
- Place the ground beef in another bowl and sprinkle with the remaining salt.
- Add the almond flour mix along with the egg and parsley. Combine the ingredients with your hands. Do not overwork the beef.
- Preheat your broiler, line a large-size baking sheet with parchment paper and set aside.
- Use the beef mixture to make small meatballs (make around 20).
- Place them on the prepared baking sheet and broil for about 3 minutes until lightly browned.
- Transfer the browned meatballs to your slow cooker (do not add any fat released during broiling).
- Add the sauce ingredients to the cooker and stir, paying attention not to break the meatballs.
- Cover and cook on low for 4 hours.
- Once cooked, allow to cool slightly and serve.

Balsamic Short Ribs

IMAGE SOURCE: Pixabay

Servings: 4, Calories: 281.0, Total Fat: 15.1 g, Saturated Fat: 7.0 g, Carbs: 6.7 g, Sugar: 0.0 g, Protein: 26.8 g

Ingredients:
4-5 bone-in beef short ribs
Salt, to taste
Black pepper, to taste
¼ cup balsamic vinegar
2 tsp mustard
½ cup beef broth
1 Tbsp ghee
1 yellow onion, thickly sliced

1 bay leaf
2 sprigs fresh rosemary

Instructions:

- Season the ribs with salt and pepper and set aside.
- Combine the balsamic vinegar, mustard, and stock and set aside.
- Preheat a large-size pan, add the ghee and once melted, add the ribs to the pan. Working in batches, fry for about 10-15 minutes and when browned, transfer to a plate.
- Add the onion to the same pan along with the vinegar mix and the bay leaf and rosemary. Scrape the bottom to incorporate any browned bits into the mixture.
- When it begins to simmer, pour the mixture into the cooker. Cook on low for 7-8 hours or on high for 4 hours.
- Once the meat is cooked through, take it out of the cooker and serve warm, drizzle with the cooking liquid and with mashed parsnip or sautéed kale.

Pot Roast

IMAGE SOURCE: Pixabay

Servings: 6, Calories: 988.2, Total Fat: 58.9 g, Saturated Fat: 4.3 g, Carbs: 21.1 g, Sugar: 3.8 g, Protein: 87.8 g

Ingredients:
2 onions, quartered
2 cloves garlic, crushed
2 celery sticks, chopped
1 lb small potatoes, unpeeled and washed
4 lb boneless chuck roast
Salt, to taste
Black pepper, to taste
1 lb carrots, peeled
3 bay leaves
1 sprig of thyme
1 cup water
2 Tbsp arrowroot powder, combined with 2 tablespoons cold water

Instructions:

- Add the onions, garlic, celery, and half the potatoes to your slow cooker.
- Top with the beef and season with salt and pepper. Add the remaining potatoes along with the carrots and tuck the bay leaves and thyme along the sides of the beef.
- Pour in the water and cook on high for about 3-4 hours.
- When the cooking time is over, pour the liquid out of the cooker into a pan. Add the arrowroot mixture and cook on medium, stirring frequently.
- Once the sauce has thickened, remove it from the heat and drizzle over the beef.
- Serve the beef with the cooked veggies (you can coarsely mash them).

Sweet Potato & Beef Chili

IMAGE SOURCE: Pixabay

Servings: 10, Calories: 308.4, Total Fat: 21.7 g, Saturated Fat: 8.7 g, Carbs: 13.0 g, Sugar: 1.8 g, Protein: 15.7 g

Ingredients:
2 lb ground beef
1 onion, diced

1 clove garlic, minced
2 can (14 oz) tomato sauce
1 can (14 oz) petite minced tomatoes
2 large sweet potatoes, peeled and diced
¼ tsp oregano
3-4 Tbsp chili powder
3 cups beef broth
2 tsp salt
½ tsp black pepper

Instructions:

- Add the ingredients to your slow cooker and give it a good stir.
- Cover and cook on high for 3 to 4 hours or on low for 6 to 8 hours.
- Once done, stir well and serve warm.

Beef Encebollado

IMAGE SOURCE: Pixabay

Servings: 6, Calories: 468.2, Total Fat: 29.4 g, Saturated Fat: 2.2 g, Carbs: 4.2 g, Sugar: 0.0 g, Protein: 43.7 g

Ingredients:
2 lb lean top round beef roast
Salt, to taste
Black pepper, to taste
4 garlic cloves, thinly sliced

2 onions, thinly sliced

1 cup beef broth

2 tsp dried oregano

2 Tbsp white vinegar

1 tsp cumin

Instructions:

- Place the beef into your slow cooker, sprinkle with salt and pepper and add the garlic and onions.
- In a bowl, combine the broth with the oregano, vinegar, and cumin and pour the mixture into the cooker.
- Give it a good stir and cook covered on low for 8 hours.
- Serve warm.

Birria De Res

IMAGE SOURCE: Pixabay

Servings: 6, Calories: 473.0, Total Fat: 29.8 g, Saturated Fat: 2.2 g, Carbs: 5.3 g, Sugar: 0.5 g, Protein: 43.7 g

Instructions:
2 dried ancho chiles
3 dried guajillo peppers
2 dried pasilla chiles
1 ½ cup water

4 tomatoes, chopped
1 tsp cumin
3 garlic cloves, minced
3/4 tsp pepper
1/2 tsp salt
2 lb lean top round beef roast

Instructions:

- Add the chiles to a saucepan and heat them on medium for about 3 minutes or until fragrant.
- Pour in the water, turn off the heat and leave to sit covered for half an hour.
- Drain the chiles (don't discard the water), deseed them and add to the blender along with the tomatoes, cooking water, cumin, garlic, salt, and pepper. Blend the ingredients until smooth.
- Transfer the sauce to your slow cooker. Add the beef, set on low and cook for 6-8 hours.
- Once cooked through, shred the beef and serve warm.